LIGHT IN THE DARKNESS

DANE THOMAS

Copyright© Dane Thomas
All rights reserved.

Reproduction of the whole or any parts of the content of this book without written permission is prohibited.

Printed in the
United States of America
ISBN   9781723577529

Book Design: Dane Thomas
First Edition: 2018

This book is dedicated to my friends and family who have never failed to leave my side despite life's challenges.

Contents

Feel it 1

Be impossible to forget 2

Heartbeat 3

Fall before you rise 4

Unfixable.. 5

Be true 6

Imperfectly perfect..................................... 7

Simply live 8

Voice 9

Power of words 10

Warm or cold 11

Bottles and broken glass 12

You'll always be searching 13

Be yourself... 14

That's where you'll find her 15

Be different 16

Let it empower you 17

Strangers 18

Absence.. 19

Timing is key 20

Search lights 21
Doubts 22
You are irreplaceable 23
Burn 24
Beauty 25
World changes 26
By the sea 27
I'd choose you 28
Wishing on a star 29
You deserve more 30
Write your own story 31
Life changes 32
Battles 33
Overcoming challenges 34
Stories 35
Fear prevents happiness 36
Ice cold 37
The whole world can change 38
Let go 39
Self love 40
Strike your match 41
Hello 42

Smile 43

Expectations 44

Happiness 45

Tears 46

No longer holding on 47

Stay 48

Holding on too long 49

History 50

Wait for them 51

Finding yourself 52

Glimmer 53

Shine bright 54

Mistakes 55

You'll be wishing 56

Unforgettable 57

Moment 58

Fail 59

Untamable 60

Silence 61

Fate 62

Fix 63

If you must 64

Mismatched pieces	65
Thought of you	66
Dawn	67
Visual stories	68
Second choice	69
Shoreline	70
Souls intertwined	71
Adventure or home	72
Rhythm	73
Broken roads	74
Soul whisperer	75
Trust	76
Ambition	77
Knife wounds	78
Summer wind	79
Peace	80
Happiness will find you	81
Poison	82
Easy	83
Summer memories	84
Love yourself	85
Crash and burn	86

Beautifully broken 87
She put out the fire 88
Burning pages 89
Reckless nights.. 90
You need more 91
Broken pieces.. 92
Unashamed.. 93
Faces 94
Conquer all things 95
Understand 96
We must continue on 97
Independent... 98
Change 99
Lost 100
Broken hearted 101
Tragedy 102
Love and betrayal.................................... 103
Destruction 104
Glimpses of light..................................... 105
Reminder... 106
Moments in time 107
Cold... 108

Rain 109

Endings 110

Imperfections 111

Reflection 112

I am real 113

Plans 114

Follow your arrow 115

Average minds 116

The last time 117

Watch me burn 118

I miss you 119

My hope for you 120

Closure 121

You're beautiful to me 122

Midnight 123

Hope 124

Challenges 125

I am enough 126

Don't settle 127

Chase her 128

Flawless 129

Fragile 130

Endless 131
Lost and found 132
Farewell.. 133
Powerful minds 134
Strength 135
Rarity.. 136
Vision of happiness................................... 137
What's important 138
Solid rock 139
Breath of life 140
Sunrise.. 141
Human.. 142
Home.. 143
Brighter day 144
Glimpse of heaven 145
Fear 146
Insanity... 147
Time and place 148
Storms 149
Intertwined 150
On my mind 151
Hold on... 152

Caution	153
Heartbreakers	154
Chaos and beauty	155
Save the best for last	156
Keep searching	157
Broken things	158
Light	159
Be selfish	160
Risks	161
Madness is brilliance	162
Graceful through the pain	163
Angels and demons	164
Opportunity awaits	165
Moonbeams	166
Right and wrong	167
This all ends	168
This is who you are	169
Don't ever tear us apart	170
You'll find them	171
Still glistening	172
Walk	173
Extraordinary	174

Beautiful soul 175
You are fortunate 176
Love them or leave them........................ 177
Misguided experiences........................... 178
Brilliance or insanity.............................. 179
Live in the moment 180

Feel it

It took me years to realize, it's not about what you see, it's about what you feel. It's about the things that remind you that you're alive and free. It's about the places that make you feel like you're on top of the world, and it's about the people that never fail to make your heart race.

Be impossible to forget

Some will quickly free their mind of you and move on with their lives, but there will be others, that find you impossible to forget.

Heartbeat

And when it's right you'll know, for your hearts will beat to the same rhythm.

Fall before you rise

You will fail before you succeed. It will all fall apart before it falls together, but you see, you must overcome your weaknesses before you become strong, and you must endure the pain before you can truly understand what the meaning of happiness is.

Unfixable

Sometimes there are things in life that are too far gone to be saved, and you've got to learn how to accept that.

<u>Be true</u>

May your mind always think with the best intentions. May your words stay forever truthful. May your heart always choose to love unconditionally.

Imperfectly perfect

She made imperfection look so damn beautiful.

Simply live

The greatest thing about life is that it's unexpected. It's a chance to search for who you are. It's an opportunity to pursue your dreams. It's the possibility of falling in love, or finding the things that make you happy. Life is a thrilling adventure; so simply live.

Voice

You mustn't forget,
it only takes the voice
of one angel to silence
a thousand demons.

Power of words

You'll never understand how words can change someone's life, until you choose to speak.

__Warm or cold__

I swore to myself I'd
never lie in a bed again
where the love felt cold,
but the words "I love you"
felt warm, even if they
weren't true.

Bottles and broken glass

When we fell apart I found myself lost in a world full of whiskey bottles and broken glass, but our downfall reminded me of who I was, and I turned what I thought to be my greatest downfall, into my greatest uprising.

You'll always be searching

You'll travel near and far. You'll cross oceans, and look into the eyes of many different strangers, but the simple truth is, no matter where you go, you'll never find someone who loves you the way I did.

Be yourself

Don't ever apologize for who you are. You are one of a kind, and there is absolutely no shame in being different.

That's where you'll find her

You'll find her where the clouds make way for the brightness of the sun, where the warm air touches her skin, and where the waves crash recklessly into the sand between her toes.

Be different

You constantly think there is something wrong with you because you spend your time comparing yourself to everyone else. You aren't like them, and you'll never be like them, but that is the beauty of it; there is no one else exactly like you, and that is such an extraordinary thing.

Let it empower you

You either let pain define you, or you let it empower you; it's your choice.

Strangers

There will be people, that no matter how much time passes, always feel like home; and there will be others, that you know for a lifetime, and never cross the line of being a stranger.

Absence

Your absence simply reminded me that I deserve someone's presence.

Timing is key

It may all be falling apart, but I swear to you, when the timing is right, every one of your pieces will fall back into place.

Search lights

And just like the search lights that shine in the middle of the night, we use the glimmers of light that shine in the middle of the darkness to search for life, for love, and for our own happiness.

Doubts

Let the world have their doubts, for you have the power to prove them all wrong.

<u>You are irreplaceable</u>

You mustn't forget that you are irreplaceable, you are one in a billion, and if they can't see your worth, they don't deserve you.

Burn

You won't understand her by seeing the hell she faces, you'll understand her by seeing who she's willing to let herself burn for.

<u>Beauty</u>

She found beauty in
all things, even the pain.

World changes

The world will change, as will you, but the thing you must accept about change is, not everyone changes with you.

By the sea

You'll find a black
silhouette down by
the sea, where the
wind blows and the
waves crash recklessly,
just another girl who
lost her soul, searching
for the answers to make
her whole.

I'd choose you

If I had to relive this
life with someone,
I'd choose you;
every single time,
over and over again,
I'd choose you.

Wishing on a star

Somewhere in the world, there is someone looking up at the same moon and the same stars, praying to find someone exactly like you.

You deserve more

Someday you'll realize you deserve more than excuses and false promises, and that's the day you'll no longer commit yourself to someone who gives you nothing more than fake ass love.

<u>Write your own story</u>

Your life is your story, and you have the ability to tell that story any way you choose.

Life changes

As you grow up you see things differently, your perspective changes, your mind changes, your goals change, and sometimes you outgrow things and people, and that's okay.

Battles

These battles we fight
are meant to hurt us,
for we must learn the
brutality of pain, before
we can understand the
power of healing.

Overcoming challenges

One day all these challenges you've had to overcome will make perfect sense, for they are molding you into something absolutely incredible.

Stories

Her eyes told stories of all the love she'd lost and found, of all the nights she found her freedom under the moonlit sky, and of all the times she found herself consumed by moments in time that changed her life forever.

Fear prevents happiness

Change isn't terrifying,
it's the fear of change
that terrifies us; the fear
of the unknown, and the
fear of failure. But fear
itself keeps us from
happiness; for everything
the world has to offer,
lies on the other side of fear.

<u>Ice cold</u>

She would let her heart turn cold as ice, before she'd let a fool break it twice.

The whole world can change

As you get older you begin to realize that friendships and relationships aren't always made to last. Not everyone is cut out to endure the journey with you. There will be a time when your whole life changes because you find out who you are and what you want; but that's the joy of life, the entire world can change in a split second, and lead you to something completely different.

Let go

When I let go of you,
I set myself free, and the
course of my life changed.

Self love

You confuse yourself with someone who is unworthy, yet you are quite worthy of all the love this world has to offer.

Strike your match

Everyone struck their matches and showed her the flame, but she was the type of woman that needed to be consumed by the fire, not the type that spent her time entertaining flames she knew would quickly burn out.

Hello

Sometimes we forget
that a simple hello,
has the power to change
our entire life.

Smile

She was never afraid to show her smile, for happiness was her greatest victory.

Expectations

Their expectations won't line up with yours, but their expectations don't matter, yours do.

Happiness

Wherever you go, whoever you choose to become, I hope you never give up on your search for happiness.

Tears

And sometimes the
tears fell fast and
quick like the rain,
for it was the only
thing she had left
to wash away the pain.

<u>No longer holding on</u>

When the silence takes
over and you hear nothing
more than my footsteps as
I walk away, you will know
I am no longer holding on
to what used to be.

<u>Stay</u>

Someday there will be
someone who loves
you enough to stay,
even when the rest of the
world turn their backs
and walk away.

Holding on too long

Many different times
I let go of myself to
hold on to someone
I thought would be
there forever.

History

There is a story behind every person that explains why they are the way they are.

Every smile, every laugh, and every tear, tells things that can't be explained but must be expressed.

Wait for them

Find someone who takes you to places you have never been, someone who finds light in the darkest places, and someone who finds beauty in even the most simplistic things.

Finding yourself

You will search for years to find yourself, but the journey to figure out who you are, is a journey you must endure alone.

Glimmer

She had pieces of heaven
and glimmers of hell,
she was a good kind of bad,
but she did it so well.

Shine bright

She needs you in the same way the stars need the darkness of the night, for she needs you to truly be able to shine.

Mistakes

The mistakes you make are molding you into someone different, and helping you to understand things about yourself that must be learned through experiences.

You'll be wishing

Someday you'll wish I was
standing there by your side.
Someday you'll be willing to
give up everything just to see
me one last time. But
someday isn't today,
and I can't be left standing
here while you make
up your mind.

Unforgettable

Some people come and go and leave nothing more than a few memories that fade over time, but there will be others that change everything, and become something absolutely unforgettable.

Moment

For the whim

of a moment

you were mine,

and our hearts

ran wild and

intertwined.

Fail

I've failed a million times. I've failed at life, I've failed at love, and I've failed at everything in between.

But failing means I'm trying, and trying means I will eventually succeed.

<u>Untamable</u>

She had a heart that
ran wild, and a soul
that couldn't be tamed.

<u>Silence</u>

Sometimes silence
is more painful
than words,
but sometimes silence
is the only
way to be heard.

<u>Fate</u>

The world will always lead you to the people you need, the places you must experience, and the things you desire the most.

<u>Fix</u>

Some things end
just as quickly
as they started,
some things
don't fix you,
they leave you
broken hearted.

If you must

If you must go,
go to the place your
heart calls home.
If you must change,
change into someone
you can be proud of;
and if you must run,
run to the arms of
the one you love.

Mismatched pieces

Like a puzzle we are nothing more than hundreds of pieces that tell a story.
Our pieces are our memories, for as people come and go they take pieces of us with them, and they leave pieces of themselves behind; but at the end of it all, our mismatched pieces fit together perfectly.

<u>Thought of you</u>

The thought of you
always scares me,
because I know
exactly how we used
to love each other.

Dawn

Their bodies intertwined
in the hours of the night,
only to be separated by the
dawn of the day.

Visual stories

If you looked into her eyes you could see the stories her heart couldn't bear to tell.

<u>Second choice</u>

I tried so damn hard to make you understand that you are so much more than someone's second choice.

Shoreline

You need her like the
ocean needs the shoreline,
for even though you crash
into her and are swept away,
you will always return to her
once more.

<u>Souls intertwined</u>

And our souls intertwined with the angels and demons inside us.

<u>Adventure or home</u>

Her soul longed for adventure, yet her heart longed for a place to call home.

Rhythm

Her heart races to a rhythm that only the wildest things in the world could understand.

Broken roads

I found my happiness along the broken roads I traveled, in places I never thought I would go, and in strangers I never knew I could love.

Soul whisperer

One day you will find someone who speaks to your soul in a different way. They will be the calm to your storm, the arms that hold you through your fears, and the home your heart has been longing to find.

Trust

If you trust in one thing and one thing only, trust in the path your heart chooses to lead you.

Ambition

The things you dream
of can all come true,
if you simply have the
ambition to pursue them.

Knife wounds

And there I was, lying on the floor with knife wounds in my heart, and blood pouring out of my soul, while you walked away and closed the door.

Summer wind

And just like the wind
on a warm summer night,
she changed her direction,
and the world took her
somewhere else.

Peace

In the whim of a moment
it was over, the pain, the
heartbreak, the agony,
for I found my peace in
letting go.

Happiness will find you

This place and these people will all change. There will be things you must hold on to, and other things you must let go. You will find pain and heartbreak along these broken roads you travel, but in the end, happiness will find you.

<u>Poison</u>

Her lips taste like poison,
drown in whiskey.

<u>Easy</u>

Forever reckless with life,
and reckless with love,
for things that come easy,
aren't what dreams are made
of.

<u>Summer memories</u>

I hope you always look back
and remember me standing
in the warm summer sun
with a smile on my face,
and eyes that lit up the world.

Love yourself

And above all things, love the person you have become.

<u>Crash and burn</u>

They saw it all fall apart.
The world watched as I
crashed and burned, but
the world failed to see
how I arose from the
wreckage and pulled
the shattered pieces
back together.

Beautifully broken

Isn't it beautiful how the world can tear us apart, yet love can piece us back together.

She put out the fire

The flames of hell tried to burn her once more, but this time, she picked herself up and put out the fire.

Burning pages

I'll rip out every page of our story and burn them one by one.

Reckless nights

The nights I found myself lying in a stranger's bed were always the nights I felt so alone; wishing for things to be different when the sun arose again, yet knowing my reality was another night of being reckless with my heart and desperately searching for love that wasn't really there.

You need more

Sometimes you are forced to let someone go, not because you don't love them, but because you are not receiving the love you need in return.

Broken pieces

We find our peace in things that hold our broken pieces together.

Unashamed

I hope you find yourself completely and utterly unashamed of the person you are.

Faces

The years pass by, yet I still search for you amongst the faces of strangers.

<u>Conquer all things</u>

When you hurt from the pain, it means you are learning, growing, and beginning to conquer the things that tried to defeat you.

Understand

Some days you won't understand her, and that's okay. The best things in life aren't meant to be understood, for they must be lived and experienced to be truly loved.

We must continue on

The bird with broken
wings still sings,
the tree with broken
limbs still grows,
the person with a broken
heart still loves,
for even though we
are all broken in
different ways, we
must continue on.

Independent

An independent woman
is the most dangerous
person you will ever love,
for she will never be afraid
to walk away from love that
isn't true.

<u>Change</u>

We look to the world
when we need a change,
yet the biggest change we
need lies within us.

Lost

I hope you get lost
in all of the things that
make you feel alive.

Broken hearted

My heart will beat a thousand times before it breaks once more for you.

Tragedy

You and I were nothing more than a beautiful tragedy.

<u>Love and betrayal</u>

You can't truly understand the depth of love, until you've experienced the darkness of betrayal.

<u>Destruction</u>

How ironic it is,
we are our own
worst form of
destruction.

<u>Glimpses of light</u>

The most beautiful souls are the ones who have been broken a million times and pieced back together, for the light shines through every single part of them.

Reminder

You were my brutal reminder that pain is real, that love doesn't always last, and that people who swear they will be there forever, don't always stay.

Moments in time

It's the simplest things
that make us fall in
love with moments
in time.

<u>Cold</u>

Maybe her heart was a bit cold because she'd been burned by the warmth of a dishonest touch too many times.

Rain

There were times
I let myself get
caught in the rain,
for it never failed
to drown the things
I couldn't change.

Endings

At the end of your story, the one you call a lover, the place you call home, and the things that make you happy, will all be so different.

<u>Imperfections</u>

You always chose to love me for my imperfections, and it took me such a long time to realize how important that was.

<u>Reflection</u>

Don't be the
person the world
wants you to be;
be the person you
can stare back at
in the mirror and
love unconditionally.

I am real

I don't try to hide my insecurities. I don't always have it together, sometimes my life is a mess. I don't try to be something that I am not.
I am real.
I am extraordinarily broken in the most beautiful way.

<u>Plans</u>

Life doesn't always
turn out as we planned,
sometimes it turns out
far more incredible
than we ever expected
it to be.

Follow your arrow

In the midst of the chaos, life will change your direction and lead you to the exact place you were meant to be.

Average minds

You struggle to fit in because you are too extraordinary to be understood by average minds.

The last time

This could be the last hello. It could be the last time you see this place. It could be the last chance to say I love you. Don't ever take these moments for granted, because this all ends.

<u>Watch me burn</u>

And that's when I knew,
I had fallen into the depths
of hell to save someone who
just wanted to watch me burn.

I miss you

I miss that crooked little smile that crossed your face every time you saw me. I miss the way your eyes lit up every time I told you I loved you. I miss the conversations we had about our future and our plans to travel the world, but most of all, I miss you.

My hope for you

I hope you find your happiness along the broken roads you travel. I hope you choose to give more than you receive. I hope you never lose faith in your own abilities, and above all, I hope you never get discouraged in the pursuit of your own dreams.

Closure

Sometimes the only closure you need is finding your happiness in someone else.

You're beautiful to me

I don't give a damn
what the rest of the
world says, you will
always be beautiful
to me.

Midnight

You can't stand the
thought of someone
else's hands on her body,
yet the clock strikes
midnight and she finds
herself alone, while you
lie in someone else's bed.

Hope

I hope your hand always
finds its place in mine,
I hope your voice always
calms my fears, and most
of all, I hope your love
for me always remains
true.

Challenges

I don't always understand why things happen. I get in my own head. I make mistakes I don't know how to fix, but I am always reminded that challenges are how we learn.

<u>I am enough</u>

I always question whether
I am enough, but the
answer always remains
the same; I will always be
more than enough.

<u>Don't settle</u>

Don't settle for anyone who falls short of being absolutely mind blowing.

Chase her

If she ever leaves, chase her, for there will never be another like her.

Flawless

We were created to be
flawless in design,
yet we are classified
as imperfect, because
the world doesn't
understand our
differences.

Fragile

Life is so damn fragile.
We find ourselves
overflowing with joy,
and in the whim of a
moment our world is
crashing down around us.
But we must remember,
we must break to become
strong, and we must rebuild
to find our happiness once
again.

<u>Endless</u>

Through pain and joy,
through good and bad,
there will always be
someone who loves
you endlessly.

Lost and found

I lost myself in people, in places, and in things I never understood; but I never truly found myself, until I had lost everything that defined who I was.

Farewell

Maybe those people that left our lives too soon fulfilled their purpose, they led us to the light at the end of the tunnel, but had to return to the darkness to save someone else.

<u>Powerful minds</u>

We tend to forget the power of our own mind.

<u>Strength</u>

You will see my strength in the midst of my disaster, for pain is what makes me strong.

<u>Rarity</u>

You are a rarity
to this world,
and that is so
damn special,
don't ever forget
that.

<u>Vision of happiness</u>

You've been searching for
happiness all your life,
yet all you've ever needed
is right in front of you,
if you simply choose to
open your eyes and see.

<u>What's important</u>

I am not for everyone.
Some will hate me, while
others choose to love me,
but what is important does
not lie within their feelings or
opinions, it lies within me,
and how I choose to love
myself.

Solid rock

Some say love

is like glass,

you fall, it breaks

it never lasts.

True love is solid

like a rock,

you fall, it holds,

all hate it blocks.

Breath of life

When your body collapses
from the pain in this world,
I will be the air that breathes
life back into your soul.

<u>Sunrise</u>

Clothes scattered across the floor, they watched the sunrise tangled up in the cotton sheets.

<u>Human</u>

I don't have all the answers,
I struggle with the confusion
of life and my own
insecurities.
I am human, just like you.

Home

Home is the place your heart feels secure.

Brighter day

Life doesn't always make sense. Sometimes the confusion can tear you apart, but the beauty of it is, beyond these challenges lies a new beginning, and a brighter day.

<u>Glimpse of heaven</u>

I will always be drawn to you, because you're my little glimpse of heaven, in a world full of hell.

Fear

Each time you let fear guide you, you stray a little bit further away from your own happiness.

<u>Insanity</u>

Call it insanity,
call it madness,
call it anything
but average,
because average
never changed
the world.

Time and place

Another place,
another time,
I'll be yours,
and you'll be mine.

Storms

The storm will end,
the dust will settle,
and you must pick
yourself up and begin
to rebuild what the
world has destroyed
around you.

Intertwined

The world turned,

the stars aligned,

and our hearts found

themselves intertwined.

On my mind

There are times you cross my mind, and for a few short seconds I relive what used to be.

<u>Hold on</u>

If the world tries to separate us, I hope you choose to never let me go.

<u>Caution</u>

Beware of the people
that love your body,
but don't love your mind.

<u>Heartbreakers</u>

There will be someone whom you try your damnedest to make love you, but they never will. They will greet you with a smile and leave you with tear filled eyes, but the simple fact is, they never deserved someone as extraordinary as you.

Chaos and beauty

They tore her apart for her madness, never stopping to see the beauty in her chaos.

Save the best for last

The world will change, as will you. Love will find you, and love will fail you. You will make promises that you won't keep. You will shed tears, but you will find yourself consumed in laughter at the confusion of life. You will be intrigued by what the future holds, but I swear to you, the best things are yet to come.

Keep searching

Maybe I'm just searching for something I will never find; but the unknown will never keep me from searching.

<u>Broken things</u>

The world always has a fascinating way of piecing broken things back together.

Light

You must never be afraid of what is on the other side of the darkness, for it may be the light you've been searching for.

Be selfish

Be selfish when it comes to life and love, for your happiness depends on it.

<u>Risks</u>

It's ironic all
the things we miss,
when we are too
afraid to take a risk.

Madness is brilliance

There is something quite irresistible about the madness in her brilliance.

<u>Graceful through the pain</u>

She always had the most graceful way of letting go of the things that were tearing her apart.

Angels and demons

Shatter my heart into a million pieces and you will see, I have the strength of a thousand angels, and you have the power of just one demon.

Opportunity awaits

You hold the key to the door that decides your own fate.

Moonbeams

One day you will find someone that loves you as much as the moon loves the darkness of the night.

Right and wrong

Fail. Over and over again, fail. Fail at life, fail at love, fail at happiness. Your failures will teach you what is right, and what is wrong, and what is worth holding on to, and what must be let go.

This all ends

Cherish the time you have,
for this life, this minute, and
this moment, all end.

<u>This is who you are</u>

Embrace your faults,

cherish your scars,

for these are the things

that make you who you are.

<u>Don't ever tear us apart</u>

If the world tore us
apart a million times,
I'd love you for a
million and one.

You'll find them

One day you will find someone that changes your life for the better.
They will love all of the things others failed to appreciate, and they will care about you in a way that no one has before. This is the type of person you spend your entire life searching for, but only find once.

Still glistening

She walked out of the flames of hell still glistening with beauty like she'd never been burned.

Walk

The biggest part of the battle is walking away from people who don't deserve you.

Extraordinary

I hope you aspire to be something so extraordinary the world only has the pleasure of experiencing it once.

Beautiful soul

The most beautiful soul you will ever find is one who has experienced loss but chooses to love, one who has experienced tragedy but continues to have faith, and one who has experienced failure but continues to pursue their dreams.

You are fortunate

How fortunate you are
to simply be able to live.

<u>Love them or leave them</u>

You are not meant for everyone. Love the ones who deserves your time, and leave the ones who don't.

<u>Misguided experiences</u>

We are the product of our own misguided experiences.

<u>Brilliance or insanity</u>

Some of the most brilliant minds in our society were often the same minds being judged for insanity.

Live in the moment

In the end, everyone hopes to find happiness, but we often forget that life is a journey. Life is a journey to find ourselves. It's an experiment that requires us to test out different people and different things to see what we truly love. It's an opportunity to make mistakes and learn from our experiences. Life is so much more than just searching for happiness, it's about learning to live in the moment.

Follow Dane Thomas on these social media accounts:

Instagram @ dthomasquotes
Twitter @ dthomasquotes1
Facebook @ dthomasquotes

Other books by Dane Thomas

Black and Blue: Available on Amazon.com

Printed in Great Britain
by Amazon